Live In Wonder™

Live In Wonder Press

Second Edition: 2011

Live In Wonder: Quests, Quotes & Questions To Jumpstart Your
Journey, copyright © 2009 by Eric Saperston

Library of Congress Control Number:
ISBN: 1448652081

You will be the same person
in five years as you are today
except for the people you meet
and the books you read.

— Charlie "Tremendous" Jones

Acknowledgements

A special thanks goes out to all of you who, along this magical journey, gave me a couch to sleep on, a word of encouragement, or a few bucks for gas and dog food. You folks know who you are and how much you mean to me. With love and gratitude, I thank you all.

This book is
dedicated to
my Mom.

THE QUEST

There's only one success in life, and that's to live in
such a way that a skilled mortician is going to have a very
tough time wiping that grin from your face.
—Rosita Perez—

Remember when Alice was lost in Wonderland? She
serendipitously stumbled upon the cheshire cat and
admitted innocently, "I'm lost and not sure which way
to go." With a wry grin, the cheshire cat responded with
a question of his own: "Where do you want to go?" To
which Alice responded, "I'm not quite sure."

Grinning from ear-to-ear, the insightful cat dropped
some clever wisdom and said:

"If you're not sure where you're going, then any road
will take you there."

This book is not just about taking any road. This book is about taking your road, your adventure, your journey, your quest.

Consider this bundle of pages to be your traveling companion to anyplace worthwhile. Its sole purpose is to be a guide and a tool for the discovery of your highest truth, your deepest gifts and how to use them both to be of service to the world.

Your journey begins with 'The Quest'. The basic premise of which is this: the quickest and surest way to become anything you want to be in life is to go and learn from those who have already succeeded on a path you respect and admire.

There's an old Chinese proverb that says it even more succinctly:

"To know the road ahead, ask those coming back."

My personal experience has taught me that anything you want to know, learn or be in this world is possible because everything you need to know about how to be in the world is only a cup of coffee and an inspired conversation away.

Maybe you've always wanted to make a movie, build a boat, or live in India. Maybe you want to be a rock star, start a non-profit or write a children's book; or maybe you're just curious about the meaning of life. Whatever you desire, whatever it is that's calling you from the depths of your soul, now is the time to trust that inner voice and follow the call to adventure.

An inquisitive mind and a humble heart are all the permission and credentials you'll need to call on the most powerful and passionate people whom you respect and admire. Invite them out for a cup of coffee so you can learn from their experiences and discover the common traits, motivating factors and distinguishing characteristics that have given them the strength, courage and conviction to successfully live the lives they love.

There is no shame in asking others for help. One of my first interviews was with the jolly and charismatic Donald Keough, arguably one of the most successful business leaders in the world. When I asked him what separated the doers from the dreamers, his answer changed my life forever. He had this to say: "What separates those who achieve from those who do not is in direct proportion to one's ability to ask others for help."

Here I had been spending my whole life believing in these words: "Fake it until you make it"; "Never let them see you sweat"; and, "Only raise your hand when you are sure". Meanwhile, one of the most powerful executives on the planet is telling me: "Being vulnerable isn't a sign of weakness; it's a sign of strength. Being able to say, 'Hey, I don't know. I need your help,' that's a sign of wisdom."

It might seem like an oxymoron but in truth the quickest way to have someone respect what it is you know is to admit what you don't know. You can ask for help and be a fool for five minutes or not ask and be a fool forever.

So contemplate this: whom do you respect and admire in your life? Who is doing what it is you'd like to be doing? Whose life and lifestyle would you most like to emulate? Who's transforming the world in ways you'd like to as well? Who inspires you? Look around your world. It might be a favorite aunt or uncle, a rabbi, priest or poet, a politician, schoolteacher or rock star, a truck driver, judge or astronaut, comedian, DJ, doctor, soldier or scientist.

Wherever your curiosity and heart's longing may take you, begin right now by identifying five people in the world who have a career or a lifestyle you dream of having, who are in the type of successful romantic relationship you'd like to be in or who have a mastery over a particular skill set or ideology that you'd like to learn and master yourself.

Please write their names on the lines below.

1. _____

2. _____

3. _____

4. _____

5. _____

Next, it's as simple as this: pick up the phone, knock on their door or send them an email asking if you could take them out for a cup of coffee. Let them know that they are someone you deeply respect and admire in this world; that you've recently been given or have bought a book on following your dreams; and that this book has encouraged you to meet and learn from those you respect and admire. Let them know you are endeavoring to offer the world your highest gifts and deepest truths and in order to increase your odds of a successful journey, you would like to know if it's OK to speak with them first. The purpose of your visit would be to learn from their experiences, the values they've lived by, the struggles they've endured and specifically what advice and council they would give you to better prepare yourself for the road ahead.

Some of the people you want to meet may be easier to visit with than others. Some you might never meet for a gazillion reasons, none of which have anything to do with you. Some people might meet with you after one phone call, while others might take three months of cold calling every day. Be patient and believe in yourself. You will meet the people you're supposed to meet, so enjoy the ride and learn as much as you can along the way. No one who embarks down a path they've never taken before could possibly be aware of all the challenges, pitfalls and wrong turns that lie ahead. That's OK. All you have to do is ask people more knowledgeable than you how to get to where you want to go. Then, have the willingness and resolve to listen and to act on what you learn.

Your journey may take you across the street or to the Serengeti, to Vancouver or the Vatican, to Beijing or Baghdad, to New Delhi or to a deli in New York city.

Wherever your journey may take you, gather as many tools, ah-ha moments and epiphanies you can carry in your travel satchel. When the road is long and home is far, it will be the words of those seasoned travelers you've met along the way who will keep you going on a bad day. When you find yourself doubting your ability or second-guessing your path, it will be the remembrance of those you've interviewed and their messages of encouragement that will continue to inspire you to make the impossible possible.

Also, while on this quest, consider you are the writer, director, producer and star of your own feature film. What you think, what you say, what you believe and how you behave determine the quality and trajectory of your life's journey. In every moment, consciously or unconsciously, you are writing your own personal story's narrative. And just like in the movies, if you were writing a screenplay about a particular hero and the tale of his or her adventure, you would need to write a host of supporting characters to help in the telling of that story. In Hollywood, everyone understands that supporting characters have but one critically important function: to reveal something about our hero that we may or may not already know about them. consider everyone along your journey to be a wise teacher intentionally placed along your path to reveal and to teach you something about yourself.

So study everything. Be curious. If someone challenges your beliefs and questions your intentions, thank them. Bear in mind, you are asking people you respect and admire to help you. consider for a moment that what they are saying might be actually be true and for your highest good. No matter what is said, smile and be gracious. Then, later when you are alone test out what was said with your own inner knowing. If what they said was helpful, then take it. If not, then don't. It's your journey, so trust your instincts.

Keep in mind, as you travel in the direction of your dreams, that adventures come in all shapes and sizes. Your journey might take you on a local, state or national quest. Your sojourn might even have you go global. Or perhaps you'll discover that your most significant and rewarding adventure happens when you meet another half way.

Your quest might take you to the famous or the not so famous, to introverts or extraverts, radicals or conservatives. Some of you will be called, like I was, to meet and interview heads of state, CEO's, presidents, poets, authors and artists. On the other hand, a journey across the street to talk to a neighbor over a cup of coffee is equally as noble.

Remember, whatever you need, whatever you desire, whatever problem you want to solve, the answers are only a question and an inspiring conversation away.

While on your quest, I invite you to become an emotional archeologist, digging passionately past the outer protective layers of doubt and insecurity to discover the common traits, motivating factors and distinguishing characteristics that guide and govern people to live extraordinary lives.

May you use the lessons you learn to build a supportive community through mutually spirited dialogue, as well as, to gain access to the many tools you'll need to create, design and manifest an inspired life that you love.

One last, useful insight worth sharing: Regardless of the size, scope and complexity of one's request, the universe always seems to answer in kind. Meaning whatever it is you are asking for, the universe will match it. So if you ask small, you'll get small. If you ask big, you'll get big.

So cowboy up and use your lasso to wrangle the highest star possible. Then hold on because you're in for the brightest and shiniest ride of your life.

Life is a journey. Live in wonder.

THE QUOTES

Before embarking on any worthwhile adventure, it may be wise to take a moment of pause, and consider a few road worthy points to ponder from those travelers who have gone before you, and what they have to say about the road ahead.

Remember, "If you don't know where you are going, then any road will take you there."

May the following quotes serve as a useful compass to help guide and lift your spirits during both peaceful and turbulent times.

Many years ago Oprah Winfrey was interviewed about her life and asked whether she had known that she would become one of the most powerful women in the world.

She explained to the reporter that when she was a little girl, someone asked her what she wanted to do with her life.

She answered by saying that she didn't know. She just liked talking to people.

The person quickly retorted, "well, you can't make a living doing that."

— Dr. Wayne Dyer

Your time is limited, so don't waste it living someone else's life. Don't be trapped by dogma - which is living with the results of other people's thinking. Don't let the noise of other's opinions drown out your own inner voice. And most important, have the courage to follow your heart and intuition. They somehow already know what you truly want to become. Everything else is secondary.

— Steve Jobs

It takes courage to grow
up and turn out to be who
you really are. To be nobody
but yourself in a world that's
doing its best to make you
somebody else, is to fight the
hardest battle you are ever
going to fight. Never stop
fighting.

— E.E. Cummings

Those who dance are
thought to be quite
insane by those who
cannot hear the music.

—Angela Monet

You can have anything you want—
if you want it badly enough. You
can be anything you want to be,
do anything you set out to accomplish
if you hold to that desire with
singleness of purpose.

— Abraham Lincoln

You don't get to choose how
you're going to die. Or when.
But you can decide how you're
going to live now.

— Joan Baez

There is a vitality, a life force, an energy, a quickening that is translated through you into action, and because there is only one of you in all of time, this expression is unique. And if you block it, it will never exist through any other medium and it will be lost.

The world will not have it. It is not your business to determine how good it is nor how it compares with other expressions. It is your business to keep it yours clearly and directly, to keep the channel open. You do not even have to believe in yourself or your work. You have to keep yourself open and aware to the urges that motivate you.

Keep the channel open... No artist is pleased. [There is] no satisfaction. There is only a queer divine dissatisfaction, a blessed unrest that keeps us marching and makes us more alive than others.

— Martha Graham

Unless you are willing
to walk out into the unknown,
the chances of making a profound
difference in your life are
pretty slim.

—Tom Peters

Young. Old.
Just words.

— George Burns

"There is no use trying" said Alice; "one can't believe impossible things."

"I dare say you haven't had much practice," said the Queen. "When I was your age, I always did it for half an hour a day. Why sometimes I've believed as many as six impossible things before breakfast."

— Lewis Carroll

Your journey has molded
you for the greater good, and
it was exactly what it needed
to be.

Don't think that you've lost
time.

It took each and every
situation you have encountered
to bring you to the now.

And now is right on time.

— Asha Tyson

I beg you... to have patience with everything unresolved in your heart and try to love the questions themselves as if they were locked rooms or books written in a very foreign language. Don't search for the answers, which could not be given to you now, because you would not be able to live them. And the point is, to live everything. Live the questions now. Perhaps then, someday far in the future, you will gradually, without even noticing it, live your way into the answer...

— Rainer Maria Rilke

Life isn't about finding yourself. Life is about creating yourself.

— Unknown

Often people attempt to live their lives backwards; they try to have more things, or more money in order to do more of what they want so they will be happier. The way it actually works is the reverse. You must first be who you really are, then do what you need to do in order to have what you want.

—Margaret Young

The real challenge is not to survive. Hell, anyone can do that. It's to survive as yourself, undiminished.

— Elia Kazan

The best way out
is always through.

— Robert Frost

Heroes take journeys, confront dragons, and discover the treasure of their true selves. Although they may feel very alone during the quest, at its end their reward is a sense of community: with themselves, with other people, and with the earth.

—Carol Pearson

Every great discovery I
ever made, I gambled that
the truth was there, and
then I acted on it in faith
until I could prove its
existence.

— Arthur H. Compton

Faith is taking the first step even when you don't see the whole staircase.

—Dr. Martin Luther King, Jr.

When we are upset, it's easy to blame others. However, the true cause of our feelings is within us. For example, imagine yourself as a glass of water. Now, imagine past negative experiences as sediment at the bottom of your glass.

Next, think of others as spoons. When one stirs, the sediment clouds your water. It may appear that the spoon caused the water to cloud — but if there were no sediment, the water would remain clear no matter what.

The key, then, is to indentify our own sediment and actively work to remove it.

—Josei Toda

Today you are you,
That is truer than true.
There is no one alive
who is youer than you.

—Dr. Seuss

This may sound too simple, but is great in consequence. Until one is committed, there is hesitancy, the chance to draw back, always ineffectiveness. Concerning all acts of initiative (and creation) there is one elementary truth, the ignorance of which kills countless ideas and splendid plans: that the moment one definitely commits oneself, then providence moves too. All sorts of things occur to help one that would never otherwise have occured. A whole stream of events issues from the decision, raising in one's favor all manner of unforeseen incidents and meetings and material assistance, which no man could have dreamed would come his way. I have learned a deep respect for one of Goethe's couplets: "whatever you can do or dream you can, begin it. Boldness has genius, power and magic in it." —William H. Murray

When in doubt, make a
complete fool of yourself.
There is a microscopically
thin line between being
brilliantly creative and
acting like the most gigantic
idiot on earth.
So what the hell, leap.

– Cynthia Heimel

It's a funny thing about life, if you refuse to accept anything but the best, you will often get it.

— W. Somerset Maugham

Don't let yesterday
use too much of
today.

— Will Rogers

Finish each day and be done with it. You have done what you could; some blunders and absurdities have crept in; forget them as soon as you can.

Tomorrow is a new day; you shall begin it serenely and with too high a spirit to be encumbered with your old nonsense.

—Ralph Waldo Emerson

This is the true joy in life, the being used for a purpose recognized by yourself as a mighty one; the being a force of nature instead of a feverish, selfish little clod of ailments and grievances complaining that the world will not devote itself to making you happy.

I am of the opinion that my life belongs to the whole community, and as long as I live it is my privilege to do for it whatever I can. I want to be thoroughly used up when I die, for the harder I work the more I live.

I rejoice in life for its own sake. Life is no "brief candle" for me. It is a sort of splendid torch, which I have got hold of for the moment, and I want to make it burn as brightly as possible before handing it on to future generations.

— George Bernard Shaw

I'm not funny.
What I am is brave.

—Lucille Ball

It takes courage to push yourself
to places that you have never
been before ... to test your limits
... to break through barriers.
And the day came when the risk
it took to remain tight inside
the bud was more painful than
the risk it took to blossom.

—Anais Nin

Perhaps, this very instant
is your time.

— Louise Bogan

Don't ask yourself what the world needs; ask yourself what makes you come alive.

And then go do that.

Because what the world needs is people who have come alive.

— Howard Thurman

Twenty years from now you
will be more disappointed by
the things that you didn't
do, then by the ones you did
do.

So throw off the bowlines.
Sail away from the safe harbor.
Catch the trade winds in
your sails.

Explore. Dream. Discover.

— Mark Twain

The important thing is
this: to be able at any
moment to sacrifice
that which we are for what
we could become.

—Charles DuBois

Don't listen to those who say, "It's not done that way." Maybe it's not, but maybe you'll do it anyway. Don't listen to those who say, "You're taking too big a chance." Michelangelo would have painted the Sistine floor, and it would surely be rubbed out by today. Most important, don't listen when the little voice of fear inside you rears its ugly head and says "They're all smarter than you out there. They're more talented. They're taller, blonder, prettier, luckier and they have connections. They have a cousin who took out Meryl Streep's baby-sitter. I firmly believe that if you follow a path that interests you, not to the exclusion of love, sensitivity, and the cooperation with others, but with strength of conviction that you can move others by your efforts, and do not make success or failure the criteria by which you live, the chances are you'll be a person worthy of your own respect.   — Neil Simon

First, say to yourself
what you would be;
and then, do what you
have to do.

— Epictetus

What I point out to people is
that it's silly to be afraid that you're
not going to get what you want if you
ask. Because you are already not
getting what you want. They always
laugh about that because they realize
it's so true. Without asking you
already have failed, you already have
nothing. What are you afraid of? You're
afraid of getting what you already have!
It's ridiculous! Who cares if you don't
get it when you ask for it, because,
before you ask for it, you don't have
it anyway. So there's really nothing
to be afraid of.

— Marcia Martin

He who is afraid
of asking is ashamed
of learning .

— Danish Proverb

Everything you want is out there waiting for you to ask. Everything you want also wants you. But you have to take action to get it. People who ask confidently get more than those who are hesitant and uncertain. When you've figured out what you want to ask for, do it with certainty, boldness and confidence.

—Jack Canfield

If there is something
to gain and nothing to
lose by asking, by
all means ask !

— W. Clement Stone

The one who asks questions
doesn't lose his way.

—African Proverb

Asking is the beginning of receiving. Make sure you don't go to the ocean with a teaspoon. At least take a bucket so the kids won't laugh at you.

— Jim Rohn

If you don't ask,
you don't get.

— Mahatma Ghandi

For everyone
that asketh,
receiveth.

- Mathew 7:7

Quality questions create a quality life. Successful people ask better questions, and as a result, they get better answers.

—Anthony Robbins

For years I've been speaking and writing about the fact that what we put out is always coming back to us, no exception. It's an exciting time when more students here in earth's classroom come to see this truth in every daily experience. It doesn't matter how you come to it ... just that you do. Finally, recognize that no one is responsible for your life but you. That you're creating your current and future reality thought by thought. And what you give your attention to only gets bigger and manifests itself in the world. So try to live a life focusing on what's good and what you're grateful for in order to have more goodness. ... what I know for sure: you keep asking the right questions of yourself, and the universe will unfold in ways you never imagined.

— Oprah Winfrey

The world is full
of genies waiting
to grant your wishes.

— Percy Ross

The big question is
whether you are going
to be able to say a
hearty yes to your
adventure.

— Joseph Campbell

The journey of 10,000 miles begins with a single phone call.

— Confucius Bell

THE QUESTIONS

The following questions have been written for all of us to engage in a lively and spirited dialogue with those we respect and admire.

May we all use these questions to better understand and explore the common traits, motivating factors and core values which continue to inspire ordinary people to live extraordinary lives.

If you only read these questions and that's it, then you will have missed the fundamental reason for why this book was written. The real magic happens when you use these questions to interview another.

Most of the questions are deep and thoughtful while others are lighthearted and unpredictable. By alternating your questions from serious to playful, you'll be more likely to establish an atmosphere of enjoyment, exploration and camaraderie with those you meet.

Think of these questions as icebreakers to get your dialogue started. Begin at the beginning and turn the page, or start in the middle and bounce around. If a question doesn't speak to you, don't ask it. If a question you've asked sparks another question ... wonderful. Ask that one too.

There is a lot of white space on the pages that follow. Doodle, write notes or capture answers to life's questions. This book is for you. Use it to follow your heart and live the life you've always imagined.

Whether you meet with people you know or people you don't know, you will be amazed at the responses you get and just how profoundly these questions can enrich both your life and theirs.

Fear nothing, especially rejection. Doing anything well takes patience, determination and follow-through. Keep risking, keep learning. And keep following your own call to adventure.

Remember what Mahatma Ghandi said: "If you don't ask, you don't get."

This is your journey.

Be yourself. Speak from your heart. Trust your instincts. And have fun.

What could you
achieve in life
if you decided
to become totally
and blissfully
impervious to
hostile criticism
and rejection?

when is a risk
worth taking?

what makes
you giggle?

what's unfinished
in your life
and why?

What great
thing would
you attempt
if you knew
you could not
fail?

If you could only
tattoo one word
on your body that
best captures
who you are, what
would it be and
why ?

When do you
lie to yourself?

How do you regain
your credibility
after making a
huge mistake?

what's your
favorite joke?

When, if ever, is
it okay to quit?

How much
money will
it take to
make you
happy ?

what's it like
to be you?

what are ten
things you are
grateful for ?

What are a
hundred things
you are grateful
for ?

what's your
definition of
integrity ?

On your physical body, which scar carries the most Significance and why?

what keeps
you going on
a bad day ?

A genie grants you
three wishes, what do
you ask for and why?

What is your definition
of power?

what is your
most ingenious
idea?

When was the last
time you mooned
someone, went
streaking or skinny
dipping?

what was the
greatest obstacle
you overcame
as a child?

What takes your
breath away?

what gives
you goosebumps?

who is your hero
and why?

What profession
(other than your own)
would you most
like to experience?

what's more important
to you: to be
respected or to
be liked ?

Are we human beings
having a spiritual
experience or spiritual
beings having a human
experience?

what question
are you most
afraid to ask?

what lasts
forever?

what is worth
fighting for?

what is worth
loving for?

How do you
know when you're
ready for a
long-term
committed
relationship?

When is it hardest
for you to say
"I'm sorry"?

When is it hardest
for you to say
"No"?

What are you trying
desperately to obtain
that you don't really
need in the first
place?

What's your
definition of
success ?

What is your greatest fear?

what's something
you don't want
others to know
about you?

If your life was a carnival, which ride would you be?

When someone
you love is going
through a difficult
time, what's the
best thing to do?

what did
you learn
yesterday?

where in your life
are you so passionate
that you are totally
and completely
unstoppable?

when was the last
time you asked
someone for help
and what did you
ask for ?

How do you keep
your composure
when everyone
around you is
losing theirs?

What makes you
go hmmmm ?

Seriously, when
is it best to
hold 'em, to fold 'em
or to walk away?

what is your
deepest regret?

Who in your life still needs to be forgiven?

So far in your
life what lesson
has taken you
the longest to
learn?

How do you grow
up and become
who you really
are?

what's the
purpose of life?

when all else
fails, I __?

What was the last
practical joke you
played on someone

or someone played
on you?

If who you are
is what you do,
and what you do
goes away, well
then, who are you?

What can you do
right now to
Significantly increase
your odds of making
desirable discoveries
by accident?

Where in your life
would you say you're
an arrogant, self-
absorbed jackass?

Is it ever possible
to get enough of
what you don't
need ?

What impossible
thing would you
like to make
possible?

How do you create
a vision so big -
that others will
want to be a
part of it?

what is your
most irritating
habit?

What chief complaint
do those closest to
you have about
you?

What should others
never count on
you for ?

what do you believe
in your heart,
   but cannot prove?

what are you
thinking about
right now?

what are you
afraid to let
others know
about you?

what brings
you down?

what lifts
you up?

If you believe
God exists, what
would you like
him / her to say
to you when you
reach the pearly
gates?

what's the best
thing about being
you?

what would you
like to be remembered
for?

what separates
those who achieve
from those who
do not?

What have you
started and not
finished ?

what's the greatest
lesson you've learned
about relationships?

what's the greatest
lesson you've
learned about
Family ?

what's the greatest
lesson you've
learned about
communication?

what's the
greatest lesson
you've learned
about business?

what's the greatest
lesson you've
learned about
love ?

Are you getting
up in the morning
excited and going
to bed fulfilled?

Live In Wonder ™

Live In Wonder is for the unpredictable ones, the crazies, the pioneers. It's for the adventure seekers, the risk-takers and for all those who have the courage to trust their instincts. It's for the rule-breakers and the innovators who turn "nos" into "yeses". It's for the outspoken, the clever and the resourceful. It's where people daring to blaze new trails go for refreshing wisdom, humor and inspiration. Live In Wonder is a celebration for those who get up in the morning excited and go to bed fulfilled. It's a destination for possible-tarians, visionaries and social entrepreneurs whose lives embody the positive change they wish to see in the world. We tip our hats, raise our glasses and bow respectfully in gratitude, for it is you who ignite, enliven and inspire the world.

Mahalo. Thank You. Merci. Danke. Todah. Domo Arrigato. Cheers. Muchas Gracias.

www.LiveInWonder.com

"Sprightly!"
-The New York Times

"Worth standing up
and cheering for."
-The Atlanta Journal-Constitution

"Inspirational."
-The Washington Post

Sometimes you take a trip.
Sometimes the trip takes you.

WINNER
Audience Award
ATLANTA FILM
& VIDEO FESTIVAL
2001

WINNER
Most Memorable Film
SOUTH BY SOUTHWEST
FILM FESTIVAL
2003

DVD
VIDEO

Eric Saperston is a critically acclaimed film director, producer and author, as well as an award-winning speaker and storyteller. Eric is the chief creative officer of Live In Wonder, an experiential lifestyle company on the cutting edge of communication, film, and interactive events designed to cause and create wonder in the world.

A prolific speaker, Eric has inspired audiences including Harvard, MIT, UCLA, United Way, Nike, Million Dollar Round Table, Trader Joe's, General Mills, US Bank and Procter & Gamble, among many others.

Eric has been a featured guest on The Today Show, CNN, CNN Headline News, PBS and has been written about in the New York Times, Washington Post, Wall Street Journal, Atlanta Journal Constitution, Spin Magazine, Fast Company and National Geographic.

www.EricSaperston.com

Made in the USA
San Bernardino, CA
21 February 2015